in
this
season

jenna dayle

in this season

a poetry anthology

Contents

Dedication:

This book is dedicated
to the people who stand by us
as seasons knock us to our knees
and help us up with laughter
when the pain thaws.
For me, those
2 women
and 2 men
taught me what true love
really feels like.

seasons

They change us.

Cautiously, over time,

a winter will melt

into spring

or long summer days

will fade into shorter,

bolder autumns.

One day you blink

and the harsh snow

is all gone

or the trees have turned

to shades of

magnificent deep reds,

burnt oranges and

golden yellows.

Our lives are the same.

Only our seasons don't abide

by some vague, constant

tilt of the planet.

Our seasons journey

through periods of bright happenstance,

frustrating realities, unexpected loss

and overwhelming responsibility.

Our seasons have no

clear month of the year to point out

on the calendar and say,

"well, at least it will be

spring soon."

You just look up one day

from your hard, continuous sludging,

and you realize you haven't

been dragging lately.

Those cold feelings

you thought would never leave you

have become only a small part

of everything else you are.

You're walking tall again.

Your head is tilted to the sky

and you close tired eyes towards

a now warmer sun.

Seasons do end.

And seasons do change.

And each time

we prepare deeper roots

for that next cruel winter

and trust in nature

that this, too,

will end.

In the meantime,

curl up in a warm place,

with warm people,

& wait out the cold.

winter:

when you will hold on to anything
just to keep yourself warm

You kissed me
held me
heard me
so tenderly
I felt your love.

Now
here I am
years later
waiting to feel it again
in some small way.

how I held on to that potential for years

That couch,
where we sit in ragged house coats
and sip at coffee
while we both stare at screens.
That couch carries our imprints
of the kind of comfort that you can truly trick yourself
into believing
is a good kind of comfort,
a loving kind of comfort.
Because maybe it is.
Maybe we both just enjoy the stillness
that can run between us
while we each put ourselves to the task
of working and connecting
outside of each other.
The stillness that lived here
was as golden as the sun
creeping along the wall behind that couch.
At least, it tasted golden, back then.
One quiet afternoon, I looked up
from my lit screen
to watch that comforting presence
spread along the old stained carpet,
into the kitchen,
down the hallway,
into our bedroom.
That comfort crept into every inch of this apartment.
And I thought it was good.
I thought it was solace.
I thought it was contentment.
I thought it was love.

turns out it was just silence

I thought this was happiness:
this not being alone.

I thought my purpose could be found in him

Those bunches of colorful flowers
turned to cheap cards
and forgotten words.
The nicknames we whispered
in each other's direction
morphed into real names
on real days.
The mornings
spent watching the sun rise
faded to evenings we forgot
to be together at sunset.
Coffee became solo.
Dates became obligations.
Jobs became escapes.
Friends became separate.
Still,
we held on to this life
of less than.

the beginning felt like a fantasy at the end

I spent nights
whispering
to your sleeping back,
hoping
you'd somehow wake up
and understand
my words
better.

you never did

I feared what would happen
after I voiced these things to you,
so I just didn't voice them.

~~when you asked why I didn't tell you this before~~
when my fear was stronger than my voice

My feet flat on the floor,
eyes on my lap,
my voice low.
We have guests here
and I want to bury the shame
that is my dying love
and your disappearing fidelity.
Again.
It happened again.
I figured it out.
Again.
I'm the one being honest here
but only with you.
Hush, you, I whisper,
no one should hear this but us.
We both know
we will stay here.
Again.
On the edge of the bed,
on the edge of our relationship.
Always teetering, still wavering,
not yet ready to risk a new life.
Not until the day
we both topple over the edge
and feel alive,
again.

we found a fake kind of safety together

Taking stock:
this life,
this dissatisfaction,
this guilt.
Inside me
a voice mumbles
I forgive myself
too much
to change
the things I do.
I let things slide.
I'm weak with me.

I wasn't strong enough to change for you

My first inclination
was always
to belittle a piece of myself
to hide the raw expanse
of beautifully imperfect pieces
that wished to shine through instead.

I learned outshining you came at a cost

Paint me
with a brush
so I blend into the walls
of this
tiny apartment,
grey and white and quiet.
Hide me
in this shelter
of TV voices
and half played songs
and the stench
of old tobacco butts
& weed.
Pretend I don't live here
in your life,
in your bed.
Don't remember my name
to people you see
on the street
and in the stores.
Don't invite the
faceless friends up,
for no one is here
worth meeting, right?
Don't think anything
of not coming home
to this warm bed
2 nights a week:
only the cold, invisible woman
is lying in it anyways.
Paint me grey
and stand me in the corner
and then, truly,
forget I'm here.

I'm so camouflaged in our life, I've disappeared

I plastered on a smile,
and I got plastered,
instead of just going home
to escape these people
who I never felt
I fit in with.
I could feel the impression
I knew I made,
forever tainted
by the tales you told them
when you felt
like your insecurities would burst.
Yes, make me your scapegoat.
It doesn't matter
that you're truly ashamed of yourself.
As long as you
can stand next to me
in front of your people
and feel
like the hero of this story.

why must you make me your villain?

I explained so much in two words:
I'm late.
You explained in two words
that this couldn't possibly happen:
To you.

you were never ready for everything this body could do

I was doubled over,
hands on knees,
between the set
of double doors.
I was rushed,
sitting, breathing,
pulse racing,
into the ER.
I felt no shame
of this body
as they stripped me
behind a half-closed curtain
and gowned me.
I tried to smile,
oxygen mask
placed over my mouth,
then the IV,
and the cold electrical pads
all over my chest.
I quietly took
the shots,
the gurney ride
to the CT room,
and the doctor
who said,
"Lucky to be alive."
When stable enough
to finally be left
all alone
behind 4 walls
of soft curtains,
I wept,
blobs of tears
running into my pillow,
around my air mask,
as I reached for no one.

you didn't show up when it was death or life

I piled up the hurt,
one by one,
inside this blackened blue
bruised heart.

I never let it out
to be heard
and I know
one day
it will take it's anger out
on the insides
of this body.

my body felt the pain when I refused to

They chase me now
in small moments and
behind half-closed doors.
My breathing spikes,
the beat of my heart rises
inside this chest,
pounding against the hard bones
of my ribcage.
Every nerve ending alights
in my face,
begging me to flee
before they arrive.
I am frozen in such dark
and pitiful anticipation.
Hiding doesn't work,
and never has,
against this foe.
With each scared
and ragged breath,
they get closer.
Finally, with a gut-wrenching whimper,
they are released
and devour everything I am
and could be
tonight.

tears pursue me everywhere now

She believed
the whole wide world
was her home,
yet it was his
constricted heart
she chose to live in.

where did that wandering spirit go?

The sun still rises and sets,
whether I'm happy with myself
or not.

why am I still choosing to live like this?

He had dark thick hair,
a shy,
sparkling smile,
and I had a boyfriend.
But everyday
he said hi
and every day
I took in every inch of him.
Every inch.
The tanned skin.
The hair on his fore arms
below his rolled-up sleeves.
Those intense green eyes.
The almost nonexistent stubble.
Those wide shoulders.
The full bottom lip.
Yes.
That full bottom lip.
Until one day
I applied every inch of him
over every inch of you
when you touched me.
You noticed something more in me
that day.

I noticed I shouldn't have a boyfriend

When romance turns to
friendship,

is there still love there?

When friendship turns to
habit,

is there still love there?

When habit turns to
existence,

is there still love there?

maybe this is love or maybe this is habit

Did it claw up over
your aching back,
grasping against your wrenching hands,
as it burrowed in darkly
to that sorry heart,
to be poisoned between the cages
of your chest,
forevermore?

you let our love die inside you

While he seeks
his validation
outside of himself,
outside of us,
I'm struggling
to find it
within.

let's just live different lives now

Leaving
is like a piece being gone
in the most crucial of places
and so life
will never
quite look right
again.

I'm going to leave anyways

He carved our initials
into a tree trunk
behind my dad's work shop.
About the time we ended,
the tree grew gnarled bark
back over our letters.

nature always knows the truth of longevity

We only tasted freedom
on our withered tongues
when we stepped out of each other's arms
and into a life of saying
"we're just friends"

I just wasn't me with the label "yours"

I blinked
and the years went by.
6 years.
Nothing seemed to happen.
Nothing seemed to change.
Time can move so quick
yet the life we lived
stood us still.

we let nothing grow in our lives when we were together

I stayed long enough
to replace me with you
and love with regret.

I stayed too long

It was exhausting
on a deep,
pit-in-the-stomach,
aching in the chest,
sore feet forever
kind of level.
Loving you,
pleasing you,
holding everything I was
down, down, down,
till I was walking all over myself
along with you.
Yes.
That was exhausting.

I slept for 29 hours when you left

I ended us
so I could be all mine.

My choices,
my decisions,
my experiences.

My sadness,
my loneliness,
my fear.

I only had the power to care for one of us

I didn't give him
many pieces
of myself.

But the pieces
I gave
were the best ones
of me.

he gave them back so I could keep them

When it truly was done
and I placed the spare key
on the hall counter,
I finally,
finally,
allowed myself to be sad.
Sad for the time
I spent loving more
of another
than I spent loving the girl
living inside me.

I'm sorry, I'm sorry, sweet girl, I'm sorry

I finally
see it clearly:

I mourn
the relationship
that could have been
more than I mourn
the one that was.

that's how I let you go

I laid down,
tear stained cheek
resting softly
against the cool pillow
of our old bed.
Day light shone bright
onto the bedroom wall
yet I couldn't leave
this safe space.
He lingered
a shadow in the doorway
of the bedroom
that still belonged to us
but would soon
just belong to me.
"What is it?"
I hear the shadow's
patient voice.
He was a gentle soul.
"I don't know. Maybe..."
I sniffed,
looking away
from bright eyes.
"Maybe I was wrong. Am wrong.
Maybe I regret breaking things off.
Maybe we should stay together."
My fear is speaking for me today,
when days before,
the rest of me whispered to him
"we're over."
He glided in softly,
folding one leg under him
sitting close
to my laying form.
He reached out.
slowly rubbing circles

onto my back,
like he had in the past
on nights when life was hard,
to calm me into slumber.
"It was the right choice."
says that low, quiet voice,
a kind smile
resting on his lips.
"You were right."
Those words solidified
what was meant to happen
somehow.
Looking up at him
through tears
I knew
he felt the same as I had
those few days ago:
relief
and a sad kind of rightness.
I just nodded my head
and he continued to rub my back,
as I accepted fully
one of the greatest gifts
he'd ever give me:
my freedom.

Thank you

Your gift to me
was hindsight
and an unveiling
of the knowledge
that I could
and would, someday,
love someone
more deeply
than I ever did you.

me

There's something quiet
in the air today.
A warm whisper
of seasons shifting
and life changing.
Every gust of wind
seems to be
guiding me in the
same direction.

I had better follow it, hadn't I?

spring:

when you forever wrap and unwrap layers
trying to keep up with the confused warmth

For now,
I sit at my
little table,
sipping my
cold coffee,
and scribble
thoughts into
a journal.

the beginnings of something new

She didn't have the power
back then to see
that with that act
of release
the world would crack open
and send her more
then she'd ever dreamt of.
She didn't have the foresight
to see that.

she jumped into a new life anyways

The soup bubbles and pops
and the smell of a soon to be
blackened layer wafts
to my swollen nostrils.
I was lost in thought again
of me leaving and you,
you ready to move on to the next.
The daydreams of us
moving to music
and swaying to soft lyrics that hummed
"God only knows what
I'd be without you"
has turned into smoke again.
Now I stir the soup
with that bamboo wooden spoon
you bought
and watch a fallen tear
sizzle on the stove top.

everything is burning in this house tonight

Loneliness is temporary.
Freedom is forever.

lies I told myself when I faked it

That loud hum
of the refrigerator motor
in the night,
the sound of water
dripping from the leaky tap
in that old bathtub,
the most silent of buzzes
off the TV screen
that glares
with nothing on.
They scream at me
of the quiet
that now lives
under this roof.
They bellow to me
of houses
and people
who fill their homes with voices
instead of sounds
blaring from dead,
electric machines.
What choice
do I have
but to listen to them
murmur on
in the quiet
birthed from my own defeat
of fear over love?

the lonely nights are too loud with silence

When you're single,
you find all the unexpected places to sit in your apartment.

I cry in corners and on counters, thinking of you

It's that phone call
out of the pale blue nothingness
when my breathing,
gasp after gasp,
creates dread
and tears
and worry.
You thought
I was tired and sleepy.
What inside us
whispers the idea
to let people think
our pain is something
other than real, raw heartache?
No. No!
I hurry down the line.
Don't let me go.
Please?
This is not sleep in my voice,
it is pain.
Please stay on the line.
Can I tell you about why
my pain is here visiting tonight?
It's the "Yes,"
from the other end of the line
in your deep, steady voice,
and the healing that happens
as you're brave enough
to listen
and I'm brave enough
to show you my struggle.
It's that call out of nowhere
that let me sleep tonight.

thank you for your call, your ear, your bravery to hear me

Under the stars,
into the frigid air,
my nightie stuck
to my warm skin.
You arise
to save me
from an old flame
crawling through this home
towards me.

but who will save me from you?

He curls his lips
just so
and when he looks,
his gaze passes
through the very base of me.
He won't see me
but I see him.
His knowledge,
his passion,
rakes against my soul,
slicing deep enough
to spill
the hot embers
that set me ablaze
once more.

you never knew you reignited these words in me

It was the feel of your mouth wrapped around my two fingers that ruined me for anybody else.

and your gaze as you did it

I questioned
endlessly
all night
on those nights
if I really
adored you
or if
the feel
of large,
strong hands
trailing along
the lines
of my body
made me
feel as if
I had all
the answers
I'd ever need.

you always left me with more questions than answers

Smiling over tables
moving together
under the chaos
of shining
multicolored lights.
Watching eyebrows raise
following words
of delicious teasing
from one another.
The openness is absent
between us,
except
behind locked, closed doors.
Over and over,
moments came to say
or show you
so much love in your very presence,
only to find
the moment descend away.
I find myself,
always,
still lingering,
wishing I had said it.
Wishing I had
pushed myself to your chest,
and feel you fold me in,
no matter who looked on.
The nights
were for asking
"why?"
to my white ceiling.
Why was this ghost
of closed emotions
and unsaid words
blocking my story with you

at every turn?
Once
I realized it was you.
Another time
I realized it was me.
And yet, still,
through all the knowing smiles
all the passionate looks
all the times I felt
your warm, masculine breath
on my neck,
nothing got realized
together.

I wasn't able to give myself away and neither were you

I didn't know then
that he'd ruin me
for most other men
but that he'd also ruin
his own chances with me,
too.

you live as an enemy to your own passion

The air
through the window
is fresh
but this bed,
this bed
is the stale embodiment
of you and me.

I woke up to a new day and you were already gone

I keep doing things
I'm supposed to
and it's driving me
insane.

girl, stop reading internet advice

Raindrops
create symphonies
on my bedroom
window.
I pull the blankets
tight to myself
for the warmth.

that's when you should be here

I loved you with
everything
you never saw.

I gave you
a heart
that was invincible.

Then I blamed you
for not
seeing it.

That's on me, lover.

That's on me

Love leads you
on a path
for the blind.
When you stop
and open your eyes
to look backwards,
remember to be kind.
You couldn't see
where you were going.
You didn't know
that you were stepping
on a path littered
with crushed fragments
of your own heart.

I had to break myself to get anywhere with you

I was wild
and witchy
and he burned me
at the stake
each night
in his arms.

will there ever exist a man who holds me without burning me?

My mind plays
tricks on me.

It hears love
but it sees
leaving.

your tender words confused me

When they ask
why again?
All I can say is
every time
is worth finding out
if it's the right time
this time.

I want you more than I like to admit

"I know that, babe,"
I stumble.
"But my heart doesn't."

let me cry over us even when I knew it wouldn't last

I smear his name
in blood
upon my chest.

Why not let him taint me
one last time,
by my own hands,

before the reckoning?

the flowing of my final war paint

And something in me broke
when I finally knew
beyond a doubt
that you never
wanted to hear from me
again.

it kills me that you knew what was good for me

It's the bewilderment,
it's the confusion
as I sit
at my kitchen table,
tear stained face
buried in my hands.
It's that not-knowing animal
that gnaws from my stomach
up towards my chest
pulling out pieces of me,
examining it for flaws,
eating me alive
as I silently shake
on this hard dining room chair.
The why,
that tragedy of a word
that keeps escaping
into my head
and sometimes
in great sobs
out of my mouth.
Why?
When my hands
finally reveal my eyes,
they'll methodically gather together
the ruined carcass
of my belief
in you,
in myself
and I'll have to carry it
around like that
all broken
and mutilated
until it slowly heals back together
again
in my own hands.

this leaving of people with no explanation is torture

I struck a match
to your name
and sat
watching it devour
everything you are.

I scorched your body,
ignited your heart to ashes
and lit the world aflame
for speaking of you.

For it's much, much easier
to burn you down
then to light myself on fire.

I'm just too afraid to burn again, darling

It tore everything in me
to see her blossom
under your care.

you never tended me with such loving hands

Next time.
Maybe next time.

Until then
I'll lay lonely
in this bed for 2
hoping to fill the spot
on the other side
with a body
that responds to mine
in so much
of the same way
as his.

my hesitancy is my bedfellow

And in his still silence,
I realized,

I liked him.
Maybe I even loved him.

But that didn't entitle me

to have him.

my right person, our wrong time

Inside my head
ghosts wander,
pushing hard
to get the fuck out.
They test
every surface,
beating a path
around this body,
looking in, under,
over, all of it,
riffling through
the memories,
forcing me
to feel
what they found there
before they find
a crack
and escape
through my eyes
and down my face.

like you, tears never seem to stop trying to leave me

I feared
losing myself
in another
so much
I burned them
all away
with my touch.

"I'm better off" I lie to myself

summer:

when you swagger into the heat, burn
your skin and call it beautiful

And so life moves on
a little jump and skip
at a time.
Yesterday was bearable.
Today was better.
Tomorrow, hopefully,
will bring a real smile.

the first shift of another season changing

It happened: the moving on.
But not always when she could see it.
It happened on the days
she spent huddled under blankets
with a book.
It happened on the days
spread out on the grass
with laughter and sunshine.
It happened on the days
people asked her what happened
and she quietly laid out her truth.
It happened on the days
she had the audacity
to try something new.
It happened on the days
she once again told her friends
how she felt
and wondered with them
what would happen.
It happened on the days
someone new took her hand
and smiled sidelong at her.
It happened on the days
she felt strong and powerful enough
to do the things that scared her.
It happened on the days
spent crying on the couch,
wishing it hadn't happened at all.
Moving on just happened
while she lived each day
for what it was supposed to be.
Until she realized she had stopped
moving on and started
moving closer to herself instead.

she moved on while she kept living

Sometimes,
it felt,
there were too many pieces
to fit back together,
lovingly,
in a single day
or a single season.
She slowly guided
one beautiful
& flawed piece
back into
a mended place.

repeat, repeat, repeat

Her doubt slowly
ate her away.

So she fed it that old,
broken heart
& started again with a new one.

this one's too tough for her to chew

I become loud out of intensity.
I tell you things you don't want to hear
at times you don't want to hear it.
I keep a few things secret between myself and me.
I believe my own bullshit far too often.
I very rarely believe the words coming out of anyone's mouth.
I will sit and listen to someone causing me pain
and pretend I'm ok...
(only sometimes now, I've gotten taller in my self respect).
I get petty and self-righteous when I'm most hurt.
I wish I didn't believe the words "you're right"
meant something.
I encourage people to do things I'm scared to do.
I believe in love but I so rarely believe in relationships.
I believe my soul is, and always will be, ok.
I take long amounts of time to process how I feel.
I think I don't deserve to be understood
but I keep desperately dreaming.

will you accept these things in me that drove him away?

I don't preach positivity
and eat sunshine.

I swallow my dark moments
and, damn it,
I learn how to laugh anyways.

finding my light in my dark

What
is the point?

love.... always, the possibility of love

I can be
bold
and leather clad
and still come to you
with a
soft heart.

I'm ready to be your everything

Fire did not soak in
under my skin.
Hot water failed
to penetrate
its warmth
into my bones.
Whiskey tried its damndest
to heat my belly
during the solitude
of cold summer nights.
The fevered passion
of a lover's hot breath
on my neck
couldn't even light
my insides thoroughly.
They were just no match
to the blazing sun
burning
inside this body.

I'm ready to torch this world with my longing

When you curled me
into your chest
crooning,
"Oh,
baby girl,
shhhh."
I never realized
how safe
I could feel
with a complete
stranger.

safety existed on that night with you

Oh,
I am still human
and I will lose my heart
to hope
even when my mind
knows the outcome.

the hope that precedes each of them leaving

You think you're gonna learn me?

Think again, hotshot.

You can't learn something
that's forever evolving.

all you can do is love its wild

My joy
was suffocating.
My laughter
was fucking
offensive.

I wanted to
come at the world,
and you,
with a light heart.

But at every turn
you tried,
desperately,
to fill it
with the heaviness
of your soul.

Some humans
just can't bare
to feel
this burning
sun rise.

just let me light you up inside

I get the blonde hair
from my pop
and the eyebrows
from my momma.
That look
like I have you all figured out?
That's all me, Sweetheart.

secrets between me & Mona Lisa

When you speak to me
like this, it's clear:

you only want
parts of me,
not the whole of me.

you're too afraid of all my pieces

"Do you really think I'd do that?"
"I don't know," I whispered.
Fuck,
did you scream at my audacity,
my ability
to not quite believe you.
How could I, ex-lover,
when everything you told me
about your past
was one long story
boasting that once upon a time
you did.

I'm not your proof of goodness anymore

He's not at war with me.
He's at war with himself
and I'm standing in the blast zone.

I can't be his shield from himself any longer

I am my own shield
against the rising
of your flame.
You will not burn me
without permission.

like you've done before

When I showed you
the pure abundance
of my internal strength,

You couldn't handle
the reminder
that you felt lacking
of your own.

That's on you, lover.

That's on you

I am not a forest for you
to lose yourself
desperately in.
I ask you,
if you're lost within me,
how will you ever
fully see me?
I want to look upon you
entirely
and I want to be
viewed
in all my dark & light glory
by you.
How will that ever happen
if you've chosen
to hide yourself in my wild?

I am not your escape from yourself

"Why do you
call me
your lion?"

"Because,
I'm a lioness.
I would never choose a man
who wasn't a lion
in his own right."

I would eat them alive these days

Through wild
wind blown hair,
he saw in my face
his world
crumble to dust
and be rebuilt
by my love.

he ran from my loving destruction

Your pretty words
are a warm breeze
on my face,
caressing my cheeks
and fingering at the softness
of my hair
as my heart swells
with each mention
of your whispered
confessions:
that I
am perfect for you,
that I
was made for you,
that I
made you happier
than you've been,
lately.
Yet, your breeze softened
into nothingness,
as all weak breezes do,
leaving me
in a stillness of air,
aching with absence.
That soft breath of words dying
uncovered to me
that the woman I am,
once content
with a gentle wind
of pretty words,
deserves a storm,
a hell-fury of action
and high winds,
before she'll ever
trust again.

only a hurricane of a man could move me now

I smiled, slowly,
on a Sunday,
knowing the sound
of my lazy
shuffling feet
headed for the coffee pot
was the happiest sound
in my world.

I love all my little things

I'm cutting the apron
strings, my little men.
You can survive just
fine without me.
I have filled you with
my insights, my care
and enough affection
to last the cold evenings
on your own.

Mommy needs a
break, my darling men.
I'm confident
you can go it all alone.
If you didn't heed my words
or learn a lesson,
well, there's no one
to blame but yourself, dear.

I must go live my life
now, my sweet men.
You must go figure out
what to do with yours.
But please, don't knock on my door
when you figure it out,
I'll be gone and the
house will be cold.

I quit my job as a caretaker today

I padded from one room
to the next
flicking switches on,
watching lights spread
to all corners
of this house.
Every light is glowing
on this chill,
summer morning.
I need light today –
after a night
of darkened worry
over you.

I stopped caretaking you but I didn't stop caring

I am every woman
who came before me,
and none of them.
I follow their
trodden path,
yet forge my own.

I am heeding history & creating my own

She needed help
to fight
her demons

so she gave birth
to a hero
from her own
spirit.

heroines live within us

She lay her head down to sleep.
And it was a romantic thought
that she would fall asleep
thinking of him.

But these days,
as she fell asleep,
her free thoughts drift
to wide open spaces within her heart.
She curls into the idea
of who she's allowed to be, now,
without him living
inside her head.

Now,
she has romance in her soul,
and she falls in love each night
with the anticipation
of who she gets to be tomorrow.

I never needed a man to be romanced properly

autumn:

*when you learn to put on a sweater
and light you own fire for warmth*

Each year was the forming rings of a tree to her:

Whether grown out of
strength or struggle,
it all added
to the sturdiness
of her nature.

I grow deeper roots in the fall

Knock knock.
I lean over the bannister
craning to peek
at who knocks
so deeply at my door.
Down the steps,
turn the lock,
crack the door.
Oh, it's you, Past.
What nostalgia
have you brought
with you today?
Come in,
you know I always welcome you
through my door
time and time again.
I have a romantic heart.
I always believe
in some far-off happy future
that you promise me.
Sit with me.
I'll turn on the fireplace
and we can listen to it
crackle together
as I write and stare at you
and you quietly
remind me of
all the good times
and all the soft moments
and how it felt
to be safe and held.
Remind me again,
so I can dream tonight
of a future that never comes
from a past
I never see clearly.

Sit here till I slumber,
fitfully alone in this bed,
and then ease yourself
out the door again
into the night air,
leaving the door unlocked behind you,
as you do,
to return on some distant day
to knock and enter
once more.

I still let our past come visit me some days

Maybe?

Maybe.

It was time
to stop looking
for a home
outside of
myself.

rebuilding 4 walls of this heart

I dissolve into it all.
My strongest action
started with softening
into pain,
into love,
into fear.
My growth lies
in allowing
the breakdown
before the buildup.

my wholeness came after cracking into pieces

I don't know why I don't call you
in the middle of the night
like you've told me before
that I can.

the night seems too intimate for us

My healing will be found
as I sit with my fear
instead of trying to find
a way around it.

my path leads through the pain

He said:
Whatever you want to do is fine.

I said:
You can't leave the fate of our love just in my hands.

I've learned not to carry love alone

Someday I'll watch you open,
crack that chest of yours
down the middle,
finally see every brutal inch
of that tortured,
loving heart.
Someday I'll watch you open,
unafraid of the voice
that sprouts truth
off a freed tongue.
Someday I'll watch you open.

it never occurred to me not to believe in you

Let them toss words & cast judgement.

To the still lake
within this heart
they are but
mere pebbles.

just dying ripples upon the surface

I was always allowed
to turn around
and humbly step back
into my integrity
when I'd strayed
outside its borders.

it welcomed me back after all this time

Just let me care for you.
What about my love
makes you turn your face
and scoff
at my words?
Stop disbelieving your unworthy
of worry and thought
when I am here,
proving that wrong.

you still can't look me in the eye when I love you

I spent hours in the practice of cartography
sketching maps
to figure out my path.

Drawing roads for growth
and rivers to get me
to my peace.

I crafted each turn and direction
so I would know,
each time I felt lost,
how to make it out of the wilderness of my thoughts
and out of the criss-crossed streets
of my deep emotions.

I became a master of direction.

Only to, in my unravelling wisdom, see
that I never needed a map,
not one that is ever changing
and frustrating.

I just needed to be
where I was.

And each time
find a different route

home to myself.

my path is felt, not crafted

Your dark scruff
that I ran my fingers along
endlessly,
feeling the prickles
along my searching fingers,
over and over,
up and down,
the underside of your chin.
Your warm eyes,
hazel and soft
and creamy.
Like the coffee aroma
I inhale
each morning,
I breathed them in
and was ready
for what my day would bring.

your ease reminded me to breath softer

When I found my inner voice
and began to speak my truth,
not everyone in my life
was able to hear it.

I spoke up anyways

The dream last night
of little side walks
and broken buildings
under fog,
of changing seasons
and dim yellow
light posts.
The dream last night
of reaching behind me
knowing you're there,
and touching
your face
through the
blinding mist.
The dream last night
of walking
hand
grasped desperately
in hand
but smiles
until we round the corner
and the pavement
gives way beneath our feet.
The dream last night
of being
in the trenches
of a town
and yet still,
there you were
with me
and we were holding up
the new pieces
together.

the real dream is a partner that stays

Every moment
is a new moment
to choose again
how to show up
for myself.

no past decision decides my here & now

I am the humble traveler.

I took a step out on the road
and now I am lost.
In the most amazing way.

Lost in my own world,
discovering pieces
I didn't know were there.
Taking turns
I never thought I'd take
and bursting out into love
in ways I never thought possible.

Damn if I don't know where I'm going.

I'm not a goal chaser.
I'm a wanderer.

I pick a direction that feels right in my bones
and set course towards that horizon.

What I find on my way?

The unknown, the wide open,
the savage, the sad,
the inexplicably joyful.

I am setting out to create myself,
wherever I find it along the path.

You may not see me soon.

I'm on a journey.

you'll never see this version of me again

There's a history in me
that doesn't belong to this lifetime.

A history of howls rising into the night air
and the moon shifting the tides of the sea.

I am the grace of all that lies behind me
and the hindsight that changes all that lies ahead.

I am history and future wrapped
into a full, strong body
that can only control one thing:

this one significant life.

I'm moving ahead fully for me now

I've tied myself up
in this long red ribbon
and this sickly bow
to something I think
makes me worthy.

The bow was re-tied
time after time
first by Mom,
then by Dad,
until I could tie it myself.

For many long years
I lived and I tugged
at this tight little bow,
unsure if it was
wrong or right.

Until the uneasy pain
got so damn bad
that I took this sharp knife
and cut that red ribbon
to shreds.

untying my worth from everything

And there he stood,
untethered to everything
that used to tie him
in knots and
hold him in place.

And there she stood,
untethered to everything
that used to tie her
in knots and
hold her in place.

And now they moved
ahead of that prison
of their own making –
finally ready to find each other
in the world.

our power released us all along

I met a man
who believed
there was more
out in the air
then molecules
and oxygen.

He believed in
the energy
of the earth,
the healing
power of the
mountains and
the light that
shone within
his own soul.

With patience
and conviction
he entrusted me
with the knowledge
that there is more
to life than my
thoughts and
never more to
life than my
own heart.

good men arrived when I believed in them

I've been in this place
as time stood still around me,
watching me grow but confined,
in need of uprooting and replanting
into a bigger pot
where my feet can stretch,
where my roots can reach further depths,
where my leaves can open wide.
That kind of growth comes
from being tended,
thoughtfully,
by green thumbed hands
and I only have these pink ones.
Can these delicate fingers
really move the mountains of soil
it would take
to rebuild a new resting place
that I would call
"A new life"?

I'm taking up all the space now

If we could
only see love
in our actions,
would I be able
to see it
if I looked close
at my own?

practicing love on my own heart first

He was my
safety
in a storm.

Not because
he was a lighthouse
waiting
to guide me
home,

but because
he was willing
to throw
himself
in to the waves
and feel
the fear
with me.

so there are men willing to see me fully

Stop living like the ghost
inside my life, dear.
I feel your presence
and see you flickering
the lights
but I convince myself
that you're not
really here.
Stop haunting this old heart.
Let go.
Move on.
Somewhere
there is another spirit
that might see you
more clearly than I.

only your full transparency would make me see you again

I don't want to be a queen.
I just want to be a messy human.
I don't want to be on some pedestal,
powerful, strong and calculating.
I want to feel, cry, laugh
playfully under the stars.
I don't want to be a queen.
Just let me be a woman.

why should I be perfect for you when I am so perfectly me?

He asked me
if I wrote about him,
which ones I wrote
about him.
I'll bring honesty
to the table,
I said,
What will you bring?

maybe he'll never figure out his worth to me

In a world
of prior-warning,
I show up at his door
without a call
or a message.
I know it's a shock.
You think it awfully strange.
This crazy
confused woman.
Again?
"You said we
needed to go our own ways,"
he reminds me,
rubbing his hand
on the back of that neck
the way
he always does
when he says one thing
and feels another.
"I know what I said, Lover.
But I have writer's block."
"So?"
"So.
I need inspiration,"
I say
as I brush by him
into the house.
"Inspiration?
From me?
What are you fucking talking about?"
I turn,
hackles rising
but then softening
into those clever,
solid eyes.
"You're a mystery.

Always
a mystery.
And my words
flow best
when I'm trying
desperately
to create a story
out of you."

even in your absence, you spark a fire in me

Words,
when we find the right ones,
can be transformative.

~~they always let me fall in and out of love for you~~
they helped me become this woman

I curl into a
good book
on an Autumn day
when I could
be curling
into you
instead.

there's still room for you between these words & me

This is where
I end
and begin

as I have before
so I will
again

reborn
each time
into the woman
I am meant
to be

in this season

in this heart

honor the ends, allow the beginnings

Acknowledgements

I would first like to thank you. Yes, the spirit holding this book. The person so called by my words or the cover or whatever else drew you to purchase this work. Without your support, this would never see the light of day (and neither would the next ones). I honor you for being a part of bringing more light and creation into this world just through your purchase of a book.

I would like to acknowledge my parents for never stopping me from barricading myself in my room with a good book. It made me more of who I was and for that I can't thank you enough.

I would like to thank my big sister for my first journal which intoxicated me with not just the written word, but my own written words.

I would like to acknowledge those 4 beautiful friends who are family, who saw me through this process with kind words, hard words, whispered words and laughing words. You saw me when I couldn't see myself. You saw this long before I did. To me, that is love on a level I hadn't known yet. Without it, I may not have continued, day after day, to bleed out upon the pages of my notebooks. But I knew I had people close who knew how to show up and believe in my healing.

I would like to thank Madison Hedlund, a most extraordinary believer of humanity and wholeness. I began this book the season she entered my life. Without her soul, her teaching and her light I would not have an "Autumn" chapter yet to write of. I would still be caught somewhere in summer: forever joyful but burning internally. She taught me I am whole and my well spring runs deep and clear and strong.

I would like to thank a hundred more people – the ones who maybe didn't see me, literally, through the writing process but saw me, literally, through the seasons. The ones who let me escape my grief into their homes as if I was family, the ones who showed me I could be intense *and* fun and that both were worth loving, the ones who taught me my lessons, the ones who loved me in all the ways even if just for a season or a day, the ones who wrapped me in hugs without arms or showed me what was beyond the backroads, the ones who supported me with kind words along the way, the ones who spent hours aimlessly driving with me or sitting in the sun with a coffee. Hundreds of people who contributed to my seasons, pushed me down or held me up, stood by me or knocked me to my knees. You're my teachers, my friends, the hundred different pieces that make up my heart. You're not forgotten. Not ever. No matter where our different seasons take us. I honor you.

About the Author

Jenna Dayle is a writer, poet & teacher. She lives in Northern BC, Canada with her cat roommate, Belle. She is an avid journal writer and personal expression advocate. She loves her books till they are worn and coffee stained, for she believes anything well loved should carry the evidence in its imperfections and scars. *In This Season* is her debut poetry anthology. She is currently working on her next.

Facebook

Instagram

Pinterest

@jennadayle

Copyright © 2019 by Jenna Dayle

First paperback edition April 2019

ISBN: 978 1 7985 8799 7

*This is a work of creative memoir
and fiction poetry. Not all events are true to life.*

Made in United States
North Haven, CT
30 September 2022

24772100R00095